OLD STURBRIDGE VILLAGE

OFFICIAL COMMEMORATIVE GUIDE

BECKON BOOKS

PEACEFUL PROPERTY

The Fenno House (left), located in the Center Village, was built in 1725 and moved to Old Sturbridge Village in 1949. It is the oldest building at the Village.

A Time of Great Change

New England in the early 19th century was poised between tradition and opportunity. Fifty years after George Washington was elected the nation's first president, the region was largely comprised of agricultural communities. Yankees held annual town meetings in which they elected officials and allocated funds for education, road repair, and care of the poor. Communities were knit together by exchanges of goods and work, and virtues of diligence and thrift. Farming families could produce much, but not all, of what they needed, and rural artisans could fabricate tools and utensils for their neighbors.

The first signs of change came after power was applied to spinning cotton in the 1790s. By the 1830s, the Industrial Revolution was in full force, with water-powered spinning and weaving factories all over New England. Other factories soon began churning out everything from tacks to musket barrels, keeping pace with the explosive growth in American cities and the West. Meanwhile, transportation was transformed as new and better roads were built. These roads—along with canals, railroads, and steamboats—carried a growing amount of freight and passengers with increasing speed and economy.

WORKING WATERS
A sawmill and gristmill operated on the David Wight Millpond for much of the 1800s. In the 1950s, Old Sturbridge Village moved the Vermont Covered Bridge (pictured) next to the pond.

In the countryside, things were also changing on family farms. While a family could still make a living on 75 to 150 acres, more households were supporting themselves away from the farm. Yankee farmwives continued to bake bread at home, but they were using cheaper wheat flour from western New York or Ohio. Cash was beginning to replace the more cumbersome system of credit, debit, and exchange, and the advent of factory-made cotton and woolen goods would make spinning and weaving at home seem like curious old traditions. As rural New Englanders would soon discover, a new era was upon them.

FORWARD, MARCH
This toy soldier, circa 1840, is part of Old Sturbridge Village's collection of artifacts. A wire handle on the base activates its arms.

DID *You* KNOW?

Early stagecoaches had to stop every 10 miles or so to pick up passengers and to swap out tired horses. This "staging" of fresh animals is how stagecoaches got their name.

STAGING HISTORY

This stagecoach is a replica of a Concord stagecoach, made in the early 1800s by Abbot & Downing Coach Works in Concord, New Hampshire.

WHERE EARLY AMERICA COMES TO LIFE

In 1935, Albert B. (A. B.) Wells of Southbridge, Massachusetts, faced a dilemma. His collection of early American artifacts, including furniture, tools, woodenware, and what he called "primitives" had filled his house to capacity. On the suggestion of his son George, and with the participation of his brothers and business partners, J. Cheney and Channing Wells, he created the Wells Historical Museum. In 1936, the Wells family purchased land in Sturbridge to create a working museum village where their artifacts could be displayed and studied in an authentic environment.

The property that would become Old Sturbridge Village was a farm that had been worked by generations of the Wight family since the 1700s. Comprised of 150 acres of sloping meadows, wooded hillsides, and land for waterpower along the Quinebaug River, the site included Wight's original 1783 house and two early 19th-century farm buildings. By 1941, the Wells family had moved at least six historical buildings onto the site, and on June 8, 1946, Old Sturbridge Village opened to the public.

Today, the Village is one of the nation's oldest and largest living history museums, portraying life in rural New England from 1790 to 1840. It includes more than 60 historic and reproduction buildings, and 60,000 early New England antiques. Costumed history interpreters ply their trades, cook, garden, and farm, while visitors survey the sites and participate in educational programs and period crafts. By presenting the work and play of daily life in early New England, Old Sturbridge Village provides an authentic and deeper understanding of the region's past.

TRICKS OF THE TRADE
Most New England villages had a blacksmith who made and repaired tools. Here, a costumed history interpreter demonstrates the blacksmith's trade.

FIELDS AND FENCES
The even lines of a rail fence were practical when farmers wanted to plant to the edge of their field. But building this type of fence was hard work, requiring farmers to dig postholes into the stony New England ground.

N NEW ENGLAND TALL CLOCKS

MOMENTS IN TIME

The Village has a collection of 60,000 artifacts used by rural New Englanders between 1790 and 1840, including a gallery of tall case or "grandfather" clocks.

QUILT-MARKING FORM

Women used this wooden pattern for marking quilt designs. Industrious and frugal, they created pieced quilts that sometimes included dozens of different printed fabrics. Women used new fabrics, scraps from making other garments, and pieces from old gowns or bed hangings. This pattern was used to outline the decorative stitching designs on quilts.

MUSICAL REENACTMENT

Members of the Old Sturbridge Village Fife and Drum Corps portray American military musicians in the early 19th century. They appear at many of the Village's special events, including Independence Day, Patriots' Day, and the Redcoats & Rebels Revolutionary War reenactment.

SCHOOL DAYS

Traditionally, schoolmistresses only taught young children in the summer term, but in the 1830s, female and male "school keepers" began to teach in the winter as well. This term often included older children who were not needed on the farm during the winter months.

TWO-HORSE OPEN SLEIGH

Winter visitors enjoy a sleigh ride around the Village Common. After the first snow of the year, New England families usually switched from carriage wheels to sleigh runners.

THE COMMON AND THE CENTER VILLAGE

The Center Village and Common at Old Sturbridge Village reveals the genteel tastes that were emerging in the early 19th century. The area is neat and trim by the standards of the time, with shade trees and ornamental gardens at some of the houses. A meetinghouse dominates the area, joined by houses, workshops, and businesses. Most homes are on small lots with outbuildings, gardens, and a few livestock.

In the 1830s, New England towns were self-governing communities that comprised approximately 30 square miles of countryside. These towns included a number of schoolhouses, a sprinkling of mills, and a center village built up around an open tract of public land called a "common." The common, or green, was used for grazing livestock and for training the local militia.

Farm families came to the center village to trade, visit, and worship. Merchants, tavern keepers, professional men, and craftsmen made their living in the center village by providing goods and services for outlying neighborhoods (and in some cases, distant markets). Many prosperous and influential families lived in the center village. They shared a growing concern about the appearance of their homes, grounds, and neighborhood.

SMALL HOUSE
Small House, top, is just 400 square feet. Couples just starting out, as well as less affluent families, including many Native Americans and African Americans, lived in homes of this size.

RIDING COACH
A stagecoach takes visitors past Fitch House, above. Trips over early New England roads were bumpy, dusty, and tiring.

EGG HUNT
Roosters and chickens roamed free in early New England villages, and with no coop, farm children had to search for eggs wherever the hens had laid them.

Asa Knight Store

DUMMERSTON, VERMONT, C. 1826 AND 1838–39

Located across from the Center Meetinghouse, the Asa Knight store represents a crucial link between the farming community and the world at large. The store was originally built as a modest one-story building. By 1838, it had grown into an imposing two-and-a-half-story emporium that stocked an expanding variety of products. Customers paid for their purchases with credit earned by selling such items as butter, cheese, palm leaf hats, and knitted socks to the storekeeper, who in turn sold them in the cities where he bought the goods to stock his shelves.

New England stores carried items from around the world, including woolen broadcloth from England; cotton textiles from England, France, and India; linens from Ireland and Central Europe; and silks from China and Italy. In addition, New Englanders could purchase teas, coffees, spices, sugar, raisins, and dyestuffs from China, Arabia, Greece, the East and West Indies, and South America. Domestic items included sheeting and shirting, calico prints, shoes, many tools, window glass, brooms, books, and paper goods, all made in New England shops. There were also garden seeds raised and sold by New England Shaker communities. Today, the Asa Knight store displays these items and more.

COMMERCE

Cash was scarce in Early America. Most store purchases were made on credit—even more so than today. Cash sales made up only about a quarter of Asa Knight's business. Without a computer to keep track of his debts, Knight had to carefully record each purchase by hand in his ledger book.

TIME TO TRADE

Families made many of the items that were brought to country stores to trade for cloth and other household products.

WHAT'S IN STORE?

Old Sturbridge Village conducted extensive research on the stock carried by country stores in the early 19th century. It then reproduced hundreds of items to display in the Asa Knight store.

Bullard Tavern

BUILT BY OLD STURBRIDGE VILLAGE, 1947

Originally called the Village Inn, the Bullard Tavern was built to serve food and beverages to visitors at Old Sturbridge Village. Today, it is named for Cromwell Bullard, who owned and operated a tavern in Sturbridge in the 1830s (now the Publick House inn and restaurant). When Bullard Tavern was built in the mid-20th century, the architectural philosophy was that buildings needed to look and feel appropriate to the time and region but did not need to be exact reproductions. Therefore, while the tavern incorporates some original materials, the building is primarily a 1940s impression of a 19th-century tavern.

Tavern barrooms were busy places in early New England. There, local men and travelers socialized over liquor and tobacco, discussing politics, farming, and current events. Some customers read newspapers or perused advertisements, while others sang popular songs or played cards and other games. Except for the tavern keeper's wife or daughters, barrooms were the domain of men; female travelers were entertained in separate rooms.

On The Table

Tavern guests were often served together at one long table. For the most part, rural tavern food was travelers' fare, served at regular hours, with meals often ending as stagecoach travelers rushed out the door to their next destination. While the quality of the food varied, most meals were substantial. For example, a full-scale New England breakfast might include ham, beef, sausages, pork, bread, butter, boiled potatoes, pies, coffee, and cider.

OPEN HEARTH COOKING
This "clock jack" rotates to evenly roast meat over the fire and was a novelty for wealthy and commercial cooks. Most people still turned roasts by hand.

GATHERING PLACE
Although the Temperance Movement of the 1830s was highly successful, local taverns were still popular gathering places.

CREAM OR SUGAR?
Frugal New Englanders gave new life to this broken earthenware creamer by soldering on a new tin handle. These antiques were called "make-do's."

Center Meetinghouse

STURBRIDGE, MASSACHUSETTS, 1832

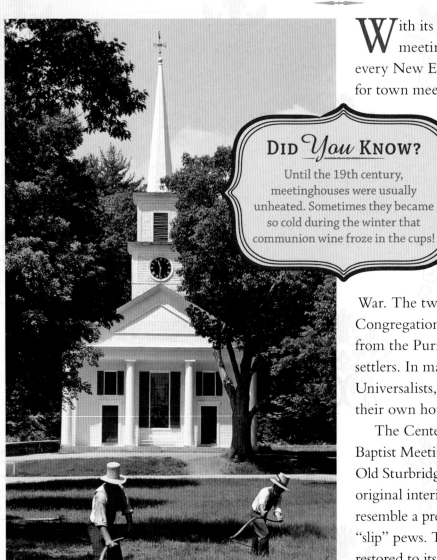

DID You KNOW?

Until the 19th century, meetinghouses were usually unheated. Sometimes they became so cold during the winter that communion wine froze in the cups!

With its steeple pointing skyward, the meetinghouse was the dominant symbol of every New England town—the gathering place for town meetings, elections, and church services. Churchgoers attended lengthy Sunday morning and afternoon services as well as midweek prayer meetings. Many 19th-century New England towns had several different meetinghouses, reflecting the region's increase in religious diversity after the Revolutionary War. The two largest denominations were Congregationalist and Baptist, both descended from the Puritan Church of the first English settlers. In many rural towns, Methodists, Universalists, Episcopalians, and Friends also had their own houses of worship.

The Center Meetinghouse was built as the Baptist Meetinghouse in Sturbridge in 1832. When Old Sturbridge Village acquired it in 1947, its original interior had been extensively modified to resemble a pre-1800s meetinghouse with paneled "slip" pews. The rest of the meetinghouse has been restored to its 1830s appearance.

GREEK REVIVAL

In New England, meetinghouses usually occupied prominent locations on the town common. These buildings were often remodeled and redecorated in rural interpretations of the Grecian style.

KEEPING WARM

Foot warmers were portable heaters, useful for winter travel or in a cold building. Inside, they contained a metal tray full of glowing coals taken from a fireplace.

MEETINGHOUSE MUSIC

This pipe organ in the Center Meetinghouse was made by Henry Pratt around 1818 for a New Hampshire meetinghouse. Originally, an organist played while a second person pumped the organ with a handle.

Cider Mill and Orchard

BROOKFIELD, NEW HAMPSHIRE, C. 1840

On a small parcel of land next to the barnyard of the Salem Towne House sits the apple orchard. Just beyond it is the Cider Mill, one of the few in New England that has survived. The building still boasts an original cider press with massive oak screws.

Cider mills operated throughout New England in September and October, converting most of the region's apple crops into cider using horse-powered crushers and hand-operated screw presses. After bringing barrels of cider home to their cellars, New England farmers intentionally let it turn "hard," or alcoholic, to preserve it. Cider was the region's most common beverage.

DID *You* KNOW?

Most early New Englanders drank cider, with the average farm family making over 300 gallons of it a year. President John Adams began each day with a glass of hard cider.

PRESERVING THE APPLE HARVEST

Making cider was just one way to preserve the apple harvest. When stored in the root cellar, some apple varieties would keep for months.

HOME ECONOMICS
Women who married and raised families between 1800 and 1825 were more likely to spin and weave at home than the generation that followed. After 1825, larger quantities of domestic and imported machine-made textiles were available in rural towns.

Fenno House Textile Exhibit

CANTON, MASSACHUSETTS, C. 1725

The Fenno House textile exhibit explores cloth making in early New England. By the early 19th century, machine-woven cloth from Britain and New England's own textile factories was eliminating demand for traditional handspun and hand-woven products. But some spinning wheels were still in use, and a number of handloom weavers continued to find custom work making blankets, coverlets, and cloth.

The Fenno House is the oldest building at Old Sturbridge Village. For more than 100 years, the house had been dated to 1704. In 2006, however, the Village conducted a study of the tree-rings on the timbers used to construct the house and discovered that the wood had been cut down in 1724. This was in line with the decorative details found inside the house.

DID *You* KNOW?

By 1826, there were 400 cotton textile mills in the region. Massachusetts alone had 135 cotton factories that produced 60,000 yards of printed cotton each week.

BEST DRESSED

This child's dress (circa 1830) and other clothing from the era can provide insight into the personal, cultural, and practical preferences of early New Englanders.

COMMUNITY FABRIC

The textile exhibit, top, at the Fenno House includes hands-on displays that reveal how materials were processed and turned into fabrics.

CAPTURED FOR POSTERITY

This daguerreotype, above, of the Fenno House was taken on its original site in Canton, Massachusetts. The daguerreotype was the first commercially successful photographic process.

Fitch House

WILLIMANTIC, CONNECTICUT, C. 1737

This symmetrical Cape-style home, which has a gambrel roof and a kitchen ell off the back of the building, had several additions through about 1820. With its white picket fence, rose trellis at the door, and a colorful flower garden designed for the children in the side yard, the Fitch House suggests the prosperity of a center village tradesman. The garden's circular layout, bright blossoms, and rustic arbor of birch saplings is based on one of New England's earliest books of horticulture advice, *The Young Florist*, written by Joseph Breck in Boston in 1833.

The Fitch House also features several outbuildings, including an original corn barn from Scituate, Rhode Island, built around 1790–1820, and a reproduction woodshed, which also houses the family privy (toilet). The large reproduction barn was built by Old Sturbridge Village in 1965 and contains an exhibit, *Tools of Agricultural Change*, which displays part of Old Sturbridge Village's extensive collection of agricultural tools and equipment.

EARLY VISITORS
When Old Sturbridge Village first opened in 1946, visitors could tour by car. This 1949 Mercury is shown outside the Fitch House shortly before car touring was discontinued.

CHILDREN AT PLAY
Children who participate in Discovery Adventure programs can dress in 1830s costumes, play period games such as rolling hoops, and learn what it was like to be a child in the early 19th century.

Friends Meetinghouse

BOLTON, MASSACHUSETTS, 1796

The Religious Society of Friends was a small denomination in early 19th-century New England. Called Quakers, they were uncompromisingly plain in dress, speech, and manners. They practiced a distinctive style of worship and were determined to maintain the integrity of their beliefs and practices.

There were close to 100 Quaker meetinghouses in 19th-century New England, often in small Quaker neighborhoods set off from the larger community. The Friends Meetinghouse at Old Sturbridge Village was built in Bolton, Massachusetts, in 1796, and the Village restored the building in the 1950s. The steeple-less meetinghouse, with its traditional 17th- and 18th-century architectural form (the "long" side was parallel to the road), was testimony to the Quaker aesthetic of plainness and the group's cultural conservatism.

DID *You* KNOW?

Since Quakers believed in the equality of all people, they didn't have ordained ministers to lead worship, and their meetinghouses lacked pulpits or altars. Instead, when they felt compelled by the Spirit, both men and women, old and young, would stand up and speak or sing.

RELIGIOUS DIVERSITY

By the 1830s, there were 19 Quaker meetinghouses in Massachusetts. A typical rural town had three to five religious societies meeting for worship.

Miner Grant Store and Bakeshop

STAFFORD, CONNECTICUT, C. 1802

Located in the hub of the Center Village is the Miner Grant Store and Bakeshop. The store was built on the site of a previous store and apothecary that burned after an accidental explosion. In 1938, A. B. Wells purchased it and moved it to Old Sturbridge Village. The Grant Store was restored in the 1940s, but while the building features some original materials, it bears little resemblance to the original 19th-century structure.

Miner Grant, Jr., had been a young clerk in the first store during the fire and narrowly escaped with his life. His father, Dr. Miner Grant, Sr., a prosperous physician and merchant, purchased and rebuilt the store. He ran it with his son, selling cloth, shoes, farm tools, flour, molasses, sugar, spices, sewing notions, tinware, glass, patent medicines, cutlery, and imported ceramics. In 1806, Grant, Jr., took over the operations, and when he died in 1850, he left the store to his nephew. The Grant Store operated well into the 20th century. Today, the Miner Grant Store is one of the museum's gift shop locations.

FASHIONABLE BONNET

This straw bonnet with fancy braid and pleated silk trim (circa 1830) is part of Old Sturbridge Village's collection. Trimmed with frills, feathers, and ribbons, wide-brimmed bonnets were popular fashion accessories for women.

FLYTRAP

This flytrap, circa 1858, had a tray that was filled with sugar water to attract flies. The flies flew in the small angled opening at left. The window in front provided light to create the appearance of an exit. When the flies tried to escape, a bag was tied over the chimney at the top.

FROM GOODS TO GIFTS

Previously a country store, the Miner Grant Store, top and above, is now one of the Village's gift shops. Modern-day visitors can find collectibles, books, toys, and games, as well as pottery made on-site.

Law Office

WOODSTOCK, CONNECTICUT, 1796

Early 19th-century lawyers were members of a growing, powerful, and challenging profession. Like their city counterparts, country lawyers spent much of their time collecting debts for prosperous citizens and drawing up leases, mortgages, property deeds, contracts, and partnerships in trade. Many also solved commerce-related problems and advocated for economic development.

Rural lawyers represented their clients at informal local courts, where they argued minor cases before justices of the peace. Four times a year, they could take other cases to the Court of Common Pleas at the county seat. Occasionally, they went before the state's Supreme Judicial Court. Many country lawyers worked in small freestanding offices like the Law Office at Old Sturbridge Village, built for John McClellan of Woodstock, Connecticut. Others worked out of rooms in their homes.

ATTORNEY AT LAW
The Law Office was moved to its current location in Old Sturbridge Village in 1965.

READING THE LAW
Before 1830, there were only two small law schools in New England: one in Litchfield, Connecticut (1784), and Harvard College (1817). Most early 19th-century lawyers did not attend law school. Instead, like tradesmen and doctors, they served an apprenticeship. After a few years of "reading the law" with a practicing attorney and using the attorney's law library when there was no pressing business, an aspiring lawyer went before a judge. If he answered the judge's questions satisfactorily, he was admitted to the bar.

SEEING CLEARLY
The Old Sturbridge Village collection contains many antique eyeglasses from the Wells family, who founded the American Optical Company in Southbridge, Massachusetts.

Parsonage

EAST BROOKFIELD, MASSACHUSETTS, C. 1748

The Solomon Richardson house, built in what is now East Brookfield, Massachusetts, is portrayed in Old Sturbridge Village as a parsonage, the home of the local minister. The Parsonage is painted white to complement the more modern Greek-Revival structures on the Common. Greek Revival was the most popular style of architecture from 1830 to 1850. This was known as a "whitening of New England," as churches, commercial buildings, and dwellings reflected the white marble facades of ancient Greek temples.

Some local churches did not provide parsonages as part of the contract, so ministers had to buy or rent their homes. A house like the Parsonage would have cost approximately $600 to $800 to buy or would have been rented for approximately $50 to $80 a year.

DID *You* KNOW?

For country ministers, the cost of living was high because they received visitors constantly and often kept guests overnight. In addition, their salaries averaged under $500—payable at the end of the yearly contract.

BABY TENDER

A "baby tender" like this was often used in busy households with small children. A baby tender was especially useful in the kitchen to keep a toddler away from a hot stove or fireplace. Similar items date back to 15th-century Europe. Child tenders, a precursor to today's playpen, demonstrate that there was some specialized "gear" designed for babies and toddlers but not in the variety available to families today.

DINNER AT THE PARSONAGE

During one of the popular "Dinner in a Country Village" special events, shown at top, diners enjoy an 1830s-style meal they learned to prepare themselves over the Parsonage hearth.

A PROMINENT HOME

The Parsonage at Old Sturbridge Village, above, is large for its day, at approximately 2,400 square feet. It was originally a 1740s farmhouse.

Printing Office

WORCESTER, MASSACHUSETTS, C. 1780

Printing required speed, dexterity, and strength. Setting type and printing were generally the work of men and boys, but women were employed in stitching and binding books. Country printers concentrated on books, pamphlets, broadsides, and forms. Newspapers were seldom profitable in small towns, but many rural printers tried to make money from them. In order to have a variety of titles for their customers, rural printers exchanged large quantities of books with printers throughout New England. Then they sold the books to country merchants, often taking store goods in exchange. By 1820, many were printing books for publishers in Boston, New York, and Philadelphia.

The Printing Office at Old Sturbridge Village was owned for a time by noted printer Isaiah Thomas. Thomas moved from Boston to Worcester during the Revolutionary War to preserve his freedom to publish. It is unlikely that Thomas printed in this building, but the association with him is important. As one of America's most successful printers, he trained many craftsmen who influenced the trade for two generations.

BUSY PRESS
Early country printers took on jobs for local customers, including printing sermons, legal forms, advertisements, and public notices, in addition to printing and binding books.

> **PUBLISHING**
> With the publication of *The Last of the Mohicans* in 1826, James Fenimore Cooper became the first professional American novelist. Still, few country folk read novels for pleasure, and rural printers rarely produced them. In the countryside, the most popular books were textbooks, religious works, almanacs, and a smattering of "how-to" guides.

EARLY LITERACY
Printing offices, such as this one, were important to the region's highly literate population. In New England in the 1830s, more people read books and newspapers than anywhere else in the country.

NO SMALL TASK
Old Sturbridge Village interpreters built the Small House using period techniques and materials. Visitors were able to watch the building's progress.

DID *You* KNOW?
One in four families in central and southern New England lived in homes that were less than 600 square feet. A family of nine or more might have lived together in these small spaces.

Small House

BUILT BY OLD STURBRIDGE VILLAGE, 2007

Small House is Old Sturbridge Village's newest "old" house, built with historic construction methods and materials between 2003 and 2007. The building reproduces the small homes that were common in New England in the early 1800s. Homes of this size or smaller sheltered newlywed couples, poor families, laborers, people of color, and renters.

Though small at 400 square feet, the Small House is multifunctional. The main room serves as both the kitchen and parlor, where most indoor work and social activity took place. It also includes a "turn-up" bed, which can be folded up against the wall to make more floor space. The back room behind the stairs is a bedchamber and storage space. There, a family might have stored cheeses and other agricultural products. The unfinished attic is portrayed as another storage area and sleeping space for children and other household members.

QUICK WORK

Women in the 1830s had to make the most of the day's available light, often doing needlework beside a window in the afternoon sunlight.

MODEST MEANS

The Small House helps tell the stories of the many people of early New England who lived with humble means and did their best to make a comfortable home for their families.

Shoe Shop

STURBRIDGE, MASSACHUSETTS, C. 1850

In New England, shoes were big business. After farming and textile manufacture, more New Englanders were employed in the shoe industry than in any other occupation in the 1830s.

A putting-out system for making shoes developed in eastern Massachusetts in the late 18th century, enabling manufacturers to produce large quantities of footwear. By 1825, the process had spread throughout the New England countryside. First, central shop manufacturers and storekeepers provided young women with the soft leather upper parts of the shoes to sew in their homes. Then the shoes were completed in small shops, where workmen sat at benches with their hammers, lasts, awls, and pegs close at hand. Durable cowhide shoes and boots with thick soles were shipped to Boston and then sent to such diverse places as Georgia, Ohio, Cuba, Haiti, and Chile for sale.

The Shoe Shop at Old Sturbridge Village was constructed in the mid-19th century, most likely as a shoe shop or another workshop. Up to 10 shoemakers might have rented space in a shop like this, each working to fill his orders.

PATTEN
Women wore pattens (circa 1790–1840), special footwear that enabled them to navigate unpaved roads and protect their long skirts during the muddy spring season. The combination of New England weather, unpaved roads, and long skirts apparently prolonged the use of pattens in rural areas.

A SOLE INDUSTRY
In the 1830s, Massachusetts made over 15 million pairs of shoes each year, as shown at top—more than one pair for every person in the country.

SHOE "UPPER"
Shoe pegging was the fastest technique for attaching the soles and heels to the upper parts (shown above). Fast workers could finish four pairs of "pegged shoes" a day using wooden pegs made cheaply by machine.

SHOEMAKING
While shoes for left and right feet have been common for thousands of years, the style has gone in and out of fashion over time. Straight shoes (made to fit either foot) were popular from the 1500s until the late 1700s, when lefts and rights began to return to favor, especially for dress shoes. In the mid-1800s, left and right styles became fashionable again for work shoes as well.

Thompson Bank

THOMPSON, CONNECTICUT, C. 1835

The Thompson Bank was one of a growing number of commercial banks in the 19th century that loaned money to promote rural industry and trade. These commercial banks were chartered and closely regulated by the state they were in. The Thompson Bank building originally stood on the common of Thompson, Connecticut. It was a bank from 1835 to 1893 and remained in Thompson until 1963, when it was moved to Old Sturbridge Village.

Designed in Greek-Revival style, the bank is furnished with astral lamps, a cast-iron stove with classical columns, and a regulator clock attributed to celebrated clockmaker Simon Willard. There is also a counter, cashier's desk, and a granite-walled vault safeguarded by a massive iron door.

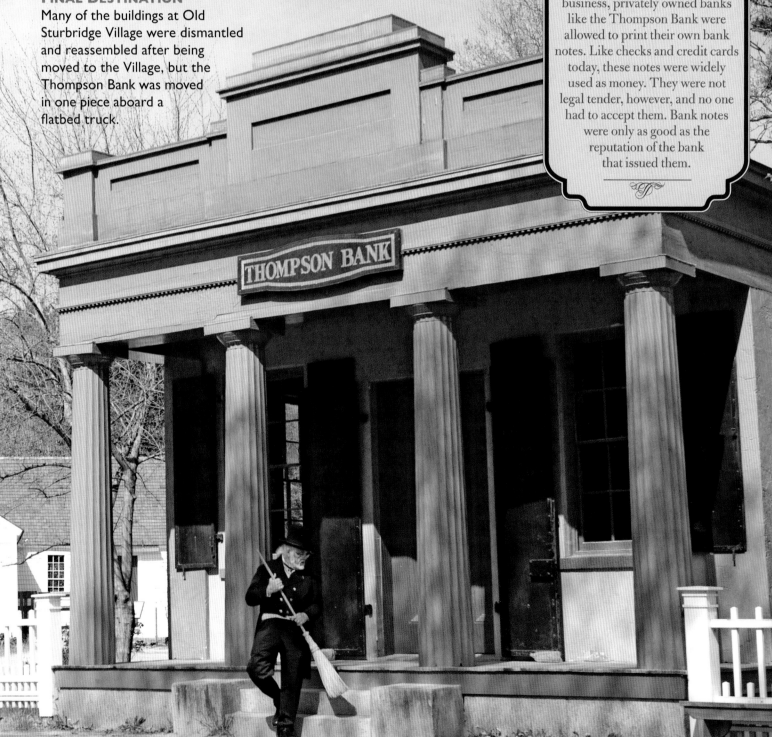

FINAL DESTINATION
Many of the buildings at Old Sturbridge Village were dismantled and reassembled after being moved to the Village, but the Thompson Bank was moved in one piece aboard a flatbed truck.

BANKING

In the 1830s, the U.S. government minted copper, silver, and gold coins, but it did not print any paper money. All coins were legal tender. Since there weren't enough coins for people to do business, privately owned banks like the Thompson Bank were allowed to print their own bank notes. Like checks and credit cards today, these notes were widely used as money. They were not legal tender, however, and no one had to accept them. Bank notes were only as good as the reputation of the bank that issued them.

Tin Shop

STURBRIDGE, MASSACHUSETTS, C. 1800–1850

The tin business in New England grew rapidly after 1820. Tin shop owners imported tinplated sheet iron from Great Britain, shaped it into a variety of forms, and distributed their finished goods wholesale through peddlers and country stores. They also sold tinware in their shops. Colanders, dippers, dish kettles, funnels, measures, and pans were in greatest demand. Other common items included lanterns, footstoves, teapots, coffeepots, tin kitchens, skimmers, and sconces.

The Tin Shop at Old Sturbridge Village is a reconfigured early 1800s shed. Here, "tinners" work with hand tools and machines that were new during the 19th century. These machines turned tinplate, made grooves and folds, and inserted wire, increasing a shop's production.

DID *You* KNOW?

The United States does not have commercial tin deposits. To this day, Americans must import what tin they need from abroad.

CASTING LIGHT

Punched tin lanterns were both beautiful and functional. The holes were punched outward to let the light out but prevent the wind from extinguishing the candle.

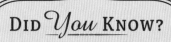

MIRACLE MATERIAL

A typical tinner in early New England had an apprentice and perhaps a couple of journeymen, depending on the size of the shop. The popularity of tinware grew during the 18th and 19th centuries. Compared with bulky and heavy woodenware and stoneware, tin was considered a wonderfully practical material—lightweight, virtually unbreakable, easy to clean, and affordable.

Town Pound

BUILT BY OLD STURBRIDGE VILLAGE

In communities with large amounts of field crops and livestock, disputes inevitably arose when one person's livestock damaged another person's crops. New England laws required farmers to fence their fields and keep farm animals from straying. Owners had to pay a fine to a town-appointed pound keeper to recover stray animals and were liable for any damage the animals had done.

The large stone Town Pound is a reproduction. Most pounds were not as substantial as this building—many were simple wooden pens.

HOLDING PENS
Each town pound was built and maintained by the community. It held livestock that was found running at large.

SPRING SHEARING
Some of the Village sheep are kept in the Town Pound. Shearing yields three to five pounds of wool per sheep.

SHEEP FARMING
Farmers in the Sturbridge area once ran flocks of 10 to 60 Merino sheep, which were imported from Spain around 1810. Noted for the fineness of their wool, they were in demand in the emerging textile industry, which paid twice as much for a Merino fleece. Due to selective breeding, today's Merino sheep no longer resemble Merinos of the 1830s. The sheep at Old Sturbridge Village are Gulf Coast Native sheep from Florida, which look like 19th-century Merino sheep and are descended from sheep brought to America by the Spaniards in the 1500s.

FARM LIFE
Farms in the 1830s usually had one pig per milking cow, since the pigs' diets primarily consisted of dairy waste from butter and cheese making.

Towne House

CHARLTON, MASSACHUSETTS, C. 1796

From its hipped roof featuring a row of monitor lights to its elegant doorway, the Towne House was built to impress. The home was constructed in 1796 and inherited by Salem Towne, Jr., and his wife, Sally, in 1825. Like his father, Towne was a businessman, land surveyor, justice of the peace, community leader, and progressive farmer. The furnishings of the sitting room reflect some of these pursuits.

The Townes ran a large and complicated household with seven children still at home in 1830, farm laborers, hired women, and sometimes visiting relatives. The first-floor kitchen of the Towne House boasts a cast-iron stove—a relatively new appliance. The house's furnishings are elegant and expensive by rural standards and are a blend of imports and New England–made goods.

Outside, the formal garden indicates the growing interest that many prosperous New England families had in ornamental gardening, with its symmetrical layout, variety of plantings, and decorative elements.

PLEASURE GARDEN
The ornamental garden at the Towne House is typical of early "pleasure gardens" and includes a variety of heirloom flowers and plants.

WORK SAMPLE
This needlework sampler was stitched by Mary Towne. In early New England, girls learned to sew as soon as they could hold a needle.

SIGNATURE STYLE
Bold wallpaper patterns and brightly colored window and floor coverings were popular in the early 1800s.

A JOINT EFFORT
Once a quilt top was pieced, friends and neighbors might be invited to a quilting party. Working together, the women would often complete the quilt in a single day.

DID *You* KNOW?
The curtains and chairs in the Salem Towne House dining room are red for a reason. Many New Englanders believed that the color red sharpened the appetite and aided in digestion.

DID *You* KNOW?

Every year, a typical New England farmhouse consumed 20 or more cords of wood—each cord measuring eight feet long, four feet high, and four feet deep—for cooking, heating, and laundry. For bathing, most people used just cold water and a cloth, and they didn't soak in tubs of hot water. Soap was used primarily for laundry.

LEARNING FROM EXPERIENCE

In early New England, each farming family's experience with crops, livestock, tools, and the cycles of the season was passed on to the next generation.

LIFE IN THE COUNTRYSIDE

In a typical New England town, some 250 farms might have been found scattered across the landscape. Sometimes a few houses, farms, and shops were clustered into small settlements with names like "South End" or "Four Corners." These mostly agricultural neighborhoods defined the immediate social and economic worlds of New England towns.

Farming was the largest sector of the economy, and it was taxing, physical labor. While oxen pulled plows and hauled heavy loads, almost every other task was accomplished by human effort, including picking stones, hoeing potatoes, cutting trees, mowing hay, spreading dung, husking corn, pressing cheese, and churning butter.

New England farmers steadily cleared their holdings, opening up forested land for grazing and hay. Native grasses were allowed to flourish in the pastures, but hayfields were sown with more nutritious "English" grasses. Farmers prepared their fields with ox-drawn plows and harrows, cultivating them through long days of hard labor. Through the winter, they felled trees for fencing and repaired tools, built sheds, chopped firewood, or worked at a supplementary trade. Caring for livestock, however, was year-round work. It required such chores as feeding and watering the animals, cleaning stalls, attending during births, shearing sheep, milking cows, and training young oxen.

INDISPENSABLE OXEN
In the 1800s, oxen were more useful than horses to New England farmers. Oxen did the heavy work on the farm and were trained to understand dozens of voice and hand commands.

ADDING ON
The Freeman Farmhouse is typical of many early houses, which had additions, or "ells," added to accommodate growing families.

Bixby House

BARRE, MASSACHUSETTS, C. 1808

The Bixby House is Old Sturbridge Village's best researched and restored home. It was home to the Bixby family from 1826 until the 1870s and was donated to the Village by the Derby family in 1974. At the time the house was donated, it still contained many original 19th-century furnishings; few modernizations had been made. Today, the walls, windows, fireplaces, architectural details, and many of the objects in the Bixby House are original, and the wallpaper, paint colors, and furnishings are close replicas.

Emerson Bixby was a blacksmith in the rural neighborhood of Barre Four Corners, Massachusetts, where he lived with his wife, Laura, and their three daughters on a one-and-a-half-acre lot. While Emerson was working at the forge, Laura and their daughters braided straw, sewed shoe uppers, raised cows, and made and sold cheese and butter. This work helped pay for home improvements, including painting the house white with bright green ("Paris Green") shutters and doors around 1840. It also enabled the family to purchase goods such as decorated tea sets and furnishings like the original Bixby family bed.

On The Table

Most New England farm families kept cows. When the weather was cool in the spring and fall, the women set out milk in large, shallow pans and waited for the cream to rise so they could skim it and churn it into butter. During the summer, when it was too hot to make butter, they preserved surplus milk by making cheese. The women stored wheels of cheese on shelves against the wall, turning them daily and rubbing them with lard in order to form a protective rind as they dried.

SNAKE RAIL FENCE

Snake rail fences, also called zigzag or Virginia rail fences, were common in 19th-century New England. Because this type of fencing was constructed without fence posts, a farmer could build it quickly; however, it used more wood and took up more ground than post-and-rail fences.

Blacksmith Shop

BOLTON, MASSACHUSETTS, C. 1810

Blacksmith Moses Wilder owned land that adjoined a stone quarry operated by his wife's cousins in Bolton, Massachusetts. Wilder built the Blacksmith Shop using some 400 granite stones from the quarry to form the walls. He was able to maintain a prosperous business making and repairing tools used in the neighboring quarry. His son, Abraham, later took over the business.

Neighborhood blacksmiths undertook several different kinds of work in rural New England, and most towns had several blacksmiths. Some specialized in producing edge tools or machinery. Others shoed horses or turned to wheelwrighting and repairing vehicles. Many did general work, repairing manufactured and imported tools, shoeing horses and oxen, and making many of the smaller items needed in the community.

FOR HOME AND HEARTH
Village blacksmiths in the early 1800s made and repaired a variety of items—iron cookware and tools for hearth cooking, as well as hoes, pitchforks, and other tools essential on a farm.

DID *You* KNOW?
We still use phrases today that began in the blacksmith's shop. For instance, "Strike while the iron is hot" means to act quickly before the opportunity is lost. Having "too many irons in the fire" means you are doing too many things at once.

IRON SHAPES IRON
Sparks fly as one blacksmith acts as the other's "striker" to get the job done faster.

Cooper Shop

WALDOBORO, MAINE, C. 1840

Originally owned by Maine artisan James Nash, the Cooper Shop is crowded with tools, casks, kegs, and pails. Coopers, or barrel makers, practiced their trade on a seasonal cycle. In the winter, they cut and hauled wood for stave stock and stacked it by the shop to dry, choosing different woods based on the goods that would be stored inside each barrel. From late March until June, coopers did farm work and made and repaired dairy containers that had shrunk or been damaged over the winter. During the summer, they worked in the fields. But at harvest time, they made barrels to store and transport grain, apples, potatoes, meal, flour, freshly pressed cider, and salted meat.

A DAY'S WORK
At Old Sturbridge Village, coopers demonstrate their craft at various times throughout the year. Traditionally, though, the account books kept by coopers indicate they practiced their trade seasonally.

FIRKIN
A firkin is a traditional unit of measure, specifically a keg that holds ¼ barrel. It is from the Dutch word for quarter, *vierdekijn*. The progression of measures went like this: pin (⅛ barrel), firkin (¼ barrel), kilderkin (½ barrel), tierce (1 ½ barrels), hogshead (2 barrels), pipe (4 barrels), and tun (8 barrels). Today, many antique dealers and collectors call any lidded bucket a firkin.

CONTAINER MAKER
The English word *cooper* is based on many linguistic roots, including the Latin word *cupa*, from which the English word *cup* is derived. A cooper is literally a maker of containers.

District School

CANDIA, NEW HAMPSHIRE, C. 1810

Long before the American Revolution, most New Englanders were required to pay taxes to provide tuition-free schools for their children. By 1800, the majority of towns were divided into districts with neighborhood schools. Schools were in session between December and March, when older children did not need to work on the farm. Younger children, too small to help with chores and likely to be underfoot, also attended school between May and August. With up to 50 students of all ages, discipline was often hard to maintain, and punishments were sometimes severe. Teachers, or "school-keepers," were usually between 17 and 25 years old and had only a district school education themselves.

New England children usually started school when they were four, learning the alphabet and then moving on to reading. At about seven, they began to study geography, followed by penmanship at nine, and arithmetic and more difficult reading between the ages of 10 and 12. Older students worked on history and grammar.

The main room of the District School features the school's original desks, which display carved graffiti from generations of schoolchildren. A stove in the center of the room provides heat on cold days, and the wood for the stove is stored in the entrance hall.

EARLY EDUCATION

District schools, pictured at left and below, were usually one-room structures. The students were called scholars and were grouped not by age but by ability. Boys and girls were seated on opposite sides of the schoolroom.

EDUCATION

Children in early New England learned through rote memorization. Before reciting, children were also taught to "make their manners": Girls curtsied and boys bowed.

Freeman Farm

STURBRIDGE, MASSACHUSETTS, C. 1808

Pliny Freeman and his family lived in this modest one-and-a-half-story gambrel-roofed house in Sturbridge in the early 1800s. During this era, farm families were endlessly busy. Besides doing the sewing and the laundry, women were responsible for raising much of the family's food. They tended large kitchen gardens, planting, weeding, and saving seeds and then harvesting and preserving the produce. They preserved the harvest by putting root vegetables in sand in the cellar, drying or smoking meats, or pickling food in brine. They also planned, cooked, and then served the household meals. Farmwomen took care of the family cows as well, making butter and cheese to provide much of the home's trade with the outside world.

Today at the Freeman Farm, work still follows the same seasonal and daily rhythms. Crops are planted and harvested, food is cooked at the kitchen hearth, animals are tended in the barnyards, and meat, butter, cheese, and produce are prepared for household use.

HEART OF THE HOME
Farmwomen worked throughout the year, raising, preserving, cooking, and serving food for their large households.

FARMHOUSE FOLIAGE
Early New England farmhouses often had fragrant lilac bushes in their dooryard, shown above. Average New England farms comprised about 80 acres and included a farmhouse, outbuildings, and fields.

KITCHEN WARES
Redware bowls and birch whisks were common kitchen staples. Even after wire whisks became available, some still preferred birch whisks for their affordability and efficiency.

On The Table

Before the age of refrigeration, people preserved meat by salting and then sometimes "smoking" it——exposing it to the smoke of a low-burning fire for a long period of time. Chambers for smoking meat could be built into the chimneys of houses or attics, or they could be freestanding structures, such as an overturned barrel.

FREEMAN BARN

The barn at Freeman Farm was built around 1830 to 1850 in Charlton, Massachusetts. It has main doors at the gable ends to allow for efficient access to cattle on one side and hay and equipment on the other. This type of barn is called a "New England–style" barn.

Pottery Shop

GOSHEN, CONNECTICUT, C. 1819

The Pottery Shop is one of the region's few remaining original structures built for creating and firing redware pottery. Outside the shed, there is a large, reproduction brick "updraft bottle" kiln for firing pots. Constructed by farmer and potter Hervey Brooks, the Pottery Shop still bears Brooks's initials on a small beam, upside down, near where Old Sturbridge Village's potters work today.

The first year that Brooks built the shed, he produced such a backlog of wares that he did not fire pottery again for eight years. From 1828 on, he made and fired one kiln load each year, primarily producing milk pans, cooking pots, and jugs, which he stamped with his name. Brooks sold some of his redware to country stores on contract, and he exchanged smaller lots with his neighbors for goods and services. Hervey Brooks also made the bricks for the Goshen, Connecticut, smoke house that now stands in the Village's Freeman Farm garden.

However, increasing competition from tinware and stoneware producers and local population decline gradually eroded demand for his goods. Brooks hung on long after virtually all of New England's redware potters had given up the craft, burning his last kiln in 1864 at 85 years old.

AT THE WHEEL
The Pottery Shop is a popular place with young visitors, who are sometimes invited to help "throw" a pot.

DID *You* KNOW?

The kiln at Old Sturbridge Village, a replica of Hervey Brooks's kiln, is made with 15,000 bricks. It stands 24 feet tall and must be heated to 1,900 degrees Fahrenheit during firing, which requires three cords of wood stoked over 24 hours. When it is fully loaded, the kiln can hold 800 pieces stacked 10 feet high.

REDWARE PITCHER
Local potters usually dug clay from the earth on their own farms, often near the bend of a river. Their wares, once commonplace, are now collector's items.

SPARKS FLY
Visitors can attend the Village's annual "Evening at the Kiln" and watch as sparks fly into the night when a year's worth of redware pottery is fired.

Woodland Walk, Pasture Walk, and River Walk

The Woodland Walk is an interpretive trail that winds through an historic woodlot. It explores the natural and cultural features of a typical wooded southern New England landscape. From the Woodland Walk, there is a short Pasture Walk across the hillside overlooking the Village Common and behind Freeman Farm. Interpretive signage and materials on the trail provide information on historic land use, fencing, and the plant and animal species found in early 19th-century New England pastures and forests. Both trails are less than one-half-mile long.

Another favorite path is the River Walk alongside the Quinebaug River, which runs through the Village. *Quinebaug* is a Native American term meaning "long, slow-moving river." During the Industrial Revolution, this gently flowing stream powered thousands of machines in scores of factories in Massachusetts and Connecticut.

AGRICULTURE

In the 1830s, as much as 75 percent of the New England landscape was cleared for agriculture and grazing. Today, a much larger percentage of the landscape is covered in forest.

PASTURE WALK
On the Old Sturbridge Village Pasture Walk, visitors can explore the unique and once common landscape of open, grassy fields used for pasturing grazing livestock. The trail also winds by vestiges of pastures now overtaken by forest.

WOODLAND WALK
The historic uses of the land and its resources by Native Americans and Euro-Americans can be traced in the plant species and other evidence found on the Woodland Walk.

QUINEBAUG RIVER WALK
Rivers and their banks have their own unique flora and fauna. Early New Englanders dammed and channeled their river resources to harness power for mills and factories.

DID *You* KNOW?
The New England countryside, with its many mill seats, was where American industrialization began.

THE DAVID WIGHT MILLPOND
The millpond was created in the 1790s by the Wight family. A sawmill operated on this pond for most of the 1800s; in 1853, a gristmill was added.

MILL NEIGHBORHOOD

The bustling center villages of New England prospered in the early 19th century because they were connected to many farms, shops, and water-powered mills in the countryside. Mills were an important part of each town's economic fabric—places where farmers brought their grain for grinding, their logs for sawing, and their wool for carding. Water-powered mills in some towns also cut nails and shingles, turned wood for furniture parts, and did other useful tasks like fulling (the cleansing and pounding of cloth, particularly wool, to make it thicker and felted together). The fulling process also finished the surface and washed out oils and dirt from processing. Most mills were owned by prosperous farmers who, for a fee, provided these essential services to their neighbors.

New Englanders harnessed waterpower from the earliest days of settlement, building mills in places where rivers or streams could be dammed or channeled to produce a fall of water. By the 1800s, most towns had a dozen or so small mills that sold little or no product. Instead, these custom mills provided one step in a process more quickly and uniformly than was possible by hand. By the early 1800s, water-powered factories began to supplement and replace the older mills, producing furniture parts, ironware, textiles, and other goods for distant markets. In 1837, the historic town of Sturbridge, Massachusetts, boasted three textile mills that made over 1.8 million yards of cotton cloth each year.

GRISTMILL
Ice and snow during the harsh New England winters often hampered the movement of the exposed Gristmill wheel.

GRISTMILL WHEEL
The hardworking Gristmill wheel has been replaced three times since Old Sturbridge Village opened in 1946.

Vermont Covered Bridge

DUMMERSTON, VERMONT C. 1870

More than 1,000 covered bridges were built in New England in the 19th and early 20th centuries; today, fewer than 200 survive. The covered bridge at Old Sturbridge Village is one of only 12 left in Massachusetts. It is distinctive because of its lattice truss design. Facing destruction from new highway construction in Vermont, it was moved to the Village in 1951. The bridge was first located 100 yards north of where it is today. It was moved to its present location after Hurricane Diane knocked it off its abutments in 1955.

DID *You* KNOW?

Bridges were covered to protect them from the elements so they would last longer. In the winter, snow was often shoveled into covered bridges so horse-drawn sleighs could glide through them smoothly.

STRUCTURALLY SOUND

The builders of covered bridges wanted to make their structures last. The roofs and sides of covered bridges kept wind, rain, snow, and sleet from the heavy beams and timbers that supported the bridge load.

ICE TONGS

Special tools were developed for ice harvesting, including large-toothed ice saws, heavy iron breaker bars, and these large ice tongs, which were used to remove ice blocks from the pond and load them onto sleds for storage in ice houses.

COLD CROPS

Ice from New England millponds became "cash crops" beginning in the early 1800s. Boston's "Ice King," Frederick Tudor, harvested and shipped ice from local ponds all over the world in the days before refrigeration.

Carding Mill

SOUTH WATERFORD, MAINE, C. 1840

Carding mills prepared wool for spinning by brushing the fibers to evenly align them. Farm families sheared, sorted, picked, and scoured wool before bringing it to the mill. Then wool was loosened in the picker to ready it for the carding machine. The "carding engines" brushed the wool into rolls for spinning or into batting for quilts. As industrialization proceeded, carding, spinning, and weaving machinery were combined in New England's expanding woolen factories. But some rural carding mills remained in operation through the middle of the 19th century, catering to a dwindling market of home spinners.

The Carding Mill at Old Sturbridge Village survived in its original condition with much of its machinery intact. It was moved to the Village in 1963. Of the hundreds that once dotted the New England landscape, it is the only water-powered carding mill to survive today.

DID *You* KNOW?

Carding machines took only 20 minutes to produce what required all day to card by hand.

WOOL PRODUCTION
Sturbridge had three carding mills by 1830, reflecting its status as a major wool producer. There, 3,000 sheep produced 7,000 to 9,000 pounds of wool a year.

Gristmill

BUILT BY OLD STURBRIDGE VILLAGE, 1938

The Gristmill was one of the first buildings constructed at Old Sturbridge Village. Built on the site of the Wight family's original gristmill, the mill is made of recycled old timbers and new lumber. The mill's massive millstones and other parts came from the Porter Gristmill in Hebron, Connecticut.

Gristmill owners served their customers by grinding grain into flour and meal for baking or provender for feeding livestock. By Massachusetts law, a miller could charge a fee or toll of 1/16th of the grain bought to him as payment for milling the rest. But rural milling was changing along with the rest of the economy; even in the countryside, cash fees were beginning to replace traditional tolls.

DID *You* KNOW?

Water-powered grain mills use ancient technology. The basic design of the gristmill was described in 23 B.C. by Roman architect Marcus Vitruvius Pollio.

ALL EARS

Old Sturbridge Village farmers grow an heirloom variety of corn called "Rhode Island white cap flint corn." In the 1830s, after a trip to the gristmill, this corn was used for animal feed, or as cornmeal for baking.

MASSIVE MILLSTONES

Millstones work like rotary scissors. One is placed just above another with grain fed between them. As the waterwheel and gears turn one stone, the grooves on its surface cross the grooves on the surface of the other stone, chopping apart kernels of grain into meal for baking.

POSTCARD FROM THE PAST

The Gristmill, which opened to the public in 1946, is pictured above in an early postcard.

Sawmill
REPRODUCED BY OLD STURBRIDGE VILLAGE, 1984

This rare water-powered sawmill—erected on the millpond site that David Wight, Jr., first created in the 1790s—is used to cut lumber for Old Sturbridge Village and other historic sites. The Sawmill is based on what had been one of the oldest surviving sawmills in the area: the Nichols-Colby Sawmill of Bow, New Hampshire, which was destroyed in a 1938 hurricane.

STURBRIDGE'S PAST
In early New England, most towns had several sawmills. There were more than a dozen in the town of Sturbridge alone by 1830.

Although the Village demonstrates sawmilling in spring, summer, and fall, rural mills were busiest during late winter and early spring, when waterpower was most abundant and the demands of farming were less pressing. Sawmill account books suggest that since it was so difficult and expensive to transport logs and lumber, mills like this one concentrated on custom production for local customers.

INCREASED PRODUCTION
One man running a sawmill could produce a thousand feet of lumber in a day, while two men using a handsaw might produce only a few hundred feet.

GARDENING

Since they didn't have modern pesticides, people in the early 1800s had to be creative when ridding their gardens of insects. One common technique was to pour hot, soapy water onto the soil one day before planting seeds, which "cooked" eggs and young insects. They also worked wood ash, chalk, tobacco snuff, sulfur, or grain husks into the soil to slow insect growth.

GARDEN VARIETY

More than 400 plants from A to Z fill the Old Sturbridge Village Herb Garden. The garden beds, laid out in three tiers, are grouped according to their use—culinary, medicinal, or household.

Museum Exhibits and the Herb Garden

MAKE AND TAKE CRAFTS
Children visiting the Hands-On Craft Center enjoy doing a variety of "make and take" activities, including making tin candle holders.

Throughout Old Sturbridge Village's 200 acres are several traditional museum exhibits, such as those in Gallery Row and the display galleries in the Visitor Center. These exhibits, which feature historical artifacts and interpretive signage, include the Glass Exhibit, Firearms & Textiles, Early Lighting, and the Herb Shed. Some of the buildings represent early shops. The Glass Exhibit resembles the first American Optical company factory in Southbridge, Massachusetts, where George Washington Wells, father of the founders of Old Sturbridge Village, began manufacturing eyeglasses in the late 1800s.

Gallery Row also features many exhibits that are popular with families. In the Dennison Building, children can see puppet shows, listen to storytelling, and enjoy the adjacent playground outside. The Hands-On Craft Center allows visitors to make candles, tin objects, and other crafts, while the Cottage is used for private events such as birthday parties and special programs.

These facilities are all clustered near the Herb Garden, a seasonal exhibit with more than 400 varieties of plants commonly cultivated in 19th-century New England household gardens or gathered from fields and woodlands. Herbs were used to flavor and preserve food, heal the sick, dye plants, and repel insects. In the Herb Garden, the herbs are displayed and grouped according to their traditional uses and labeled with both their scientific and common names.

UP IN ARMS
In the front section of the Firearms & Textiles building is a display of firearms, hunting, militia, and military equipment.

WATER LENS
One of the artifacts displayed in the Early Lighting Exhibit is a water lens. Lace makers preferred this type of lens, since it provided good illumination for their intricate work. The glass balls were filled with distilled water, and then a lamp or candle was set in the center, refracting the light and intensifying it.

Founded in 1946, Old Sturbridge Village (OSV) is one of the oldest and largest living history museums in the country, portraying life in a rural New England town of the 1830s. The Village has 60 original buildings, each carefully researched, restored, and brought to the museum site from towns throughout New England. These include homes, meetinghouses, a district school, country store, bank, law office, printing office, carding mill, gristmill, pottery, blacksmith shop, shoe shop, cooper shop, and an accurately reproduced sawmill. OSV also has several gardens with heirloom flowers and plants and a working farm with heritage breed animals.

Authentically costumed historians, called interpreters, carry out the daily activities of an early 19th-century community, and visitors can see farmwomen cooking at the hearth as well as the printer, potter, cooper, tinner, blacksmith and shoemaker at work. With four unique seasons and more than 200 acres to explore, there is always something new to see at Old Sturbridge Village.

The period of American history portrayed by Old Sturbridge Village, 1790–1840, is of major significance because it was a time in which the everyday lives of New Englanders were transformed by the rise of commerce and manufacturing, improvements in agriculture and transportation, the pulls of emigration and urbanization, and the tides of educational, political, cultural, and social change.

The Village's portrayal of the past is grounded in award-winning historical research that includes archaeology, scientific analysis of 19th-century objects and buildings, and painstaking study of letters, diaries, account books, and other documents.

Old Sturbridge Village
1 Old Sturbridge Village Road
Sturbridge, Massachusetts 01566
www.osv.org
800-SEE-1830

Acknowledgments
Ed Hood, *Vice President of Museum Program*
Deb Friedman, *Vice President of Public Program*
Tom Kelleher, *Curator of Mechanical Arts*
Ann Lindblad, *Vice President of Marketing and Communications*

Old Sturbridge Village was developed by Beckon Books in cooperation with Old Sturbridge Village and Event Network. Beckon develops and publishes custom books for leading cultural attractions, corporations, and nonprofit organizations. Beckon Books is an imprint of Southwestern Publishing Group, Inc., 2451 Atrium Way, Nashville, TN 37214. Southwestern Publishing Group, Inc., is a wholly owned subsidiary of Southwestern, Inc., Nashville, Tennessee.

Christopher G. Capen, *President, Beckon Books*
Monika Stout, *Design/Production*
Betsy Holt, *Editor*
www.beckonbooks.com
877-311-0155

Event Network is the retail partner of Old Sturbridge Village and is proud to benefit and support the Village's mission of portraying life in early New England.
www.eventnetwork.com

Photo credits
Robert Arnold, 41a; Mark Ashton, 4, 32, 36a; Susannah Bonta, 8; John Boren, 26a; David Burk, 2, 9a, 9c, 11a, 15a, 16b, 18c, 23b, 24b; 40, 42b; Frank W. Cabral, 6c; Lisa Cassidy, Cover; Webb Chappell, 10b, 21b, 24a, 25, 26c, 28b, 30, 31b, 34b, 35a, 35b, 36b, 38a, 42, 46,47a; Exclusive Image, LLC, 42a; John Ferrarone, 6a, 6b, 18b, 38b; Jeffrey Hammond, 20b, 41b; Alice Howe, 11b; Institute for the Visualization of History, 10a; Tom Kelleher, 27a; 44a; Chuck Kidd, 11c, 13, 26b, 31a; A. Konstantopoulos, 5b; Fred LeBlanc, 45a; Ann Lindblad, 23a, 24c, 29, 34c, 37, 39b,44c, 47b; Dale Lougee, 5a, 17, 18a; Walter H. Miller, 44; Thomas Neil, 7, 12a, 12c, 14, 19a, 21a, 33a, 33b; Murray Newton, 42c; Linda Orlomoski, 3b; Henry Peach, 3a, 12b, 15b, 28c; Raymona Pooler, 23b; Michael Powers, 34a; Amanda Richardson, 28a; Christian Robinson, 27b; Erika Sidor, 9b; Doreen St. John, 27c, 36c; Village Photo and Portrait Studio, 39a; Deborah Wan, 19b; Mark Wilson, 20a

ISBN: 978-1-935442-19-6
Printed in the United States of America
10 9 8 7 6 5 4 3 2 1